CITY MACHINES

CRANES

Connor Dayton

PowerKiDS press.

New York

Published in 2012 by The Rosen Publishing Group, Inc.
29 East 21st Street, New York, NY 10010

First Edition

Editor: Jennifer Way
Book Design: Ashley Drago

Photo Credits: Cover, p. 10 © www.iStockphoto.com/Rick Hyman; p. 5 Comstock/Thinkstock; pp. 6, 24 (top left) Jupiterimages/BananaStock/Thinkstock; p. 9 John Foxx/Stockbyte/ Thinkstock; p. 13 Jupiterimages/Photos.com/Thinkstock; pp. 14–15, 24 (bottom left) Sam Robinson/Digital Vision/Thinkstock; pp. 16, 20, 24 (top right) iStockphoto/Thinkstock; pp. 19, 24 (bottom right) Shutterstock.com; p. 23 © www.iStockphoto.com/Dmitry Mordvintsev.

Library of Congress Cataloging-in-Publication Data

Dayton, Connor.
 Cranes / by Connor Dayton. — 1st ed.
    p. cm. — (City machines)
 Includes bibliographical references and index.
 ISBN 978-1-4488-4959-8 (library binding) — ISBN 978-1-4488-5068-6 (pbk.) — ISBN 978-1-4488-5069-3 (6-pack)
 1. Cranes, derricks, etc.—Juvenile literature. I. Title.
 TJ1363.D39 2012
 621.8'73—dc22
                                    2010049705

Manufactured in the United States of America

CPSIA Compliance Information: Batch #WS11PK: For Further Information contact Rosen Publishing, New York, New York at 1-800-237-9932

CONTENTS

A crane is a machine. It raises and lowers heavy **loads**.

5

A person works a crane from the **cab**.

Cranes are used in building.
They lift heavy loads into the air.

The bottom of the crane is the base.

The mast rises from the base.
It is also called the tower.

13

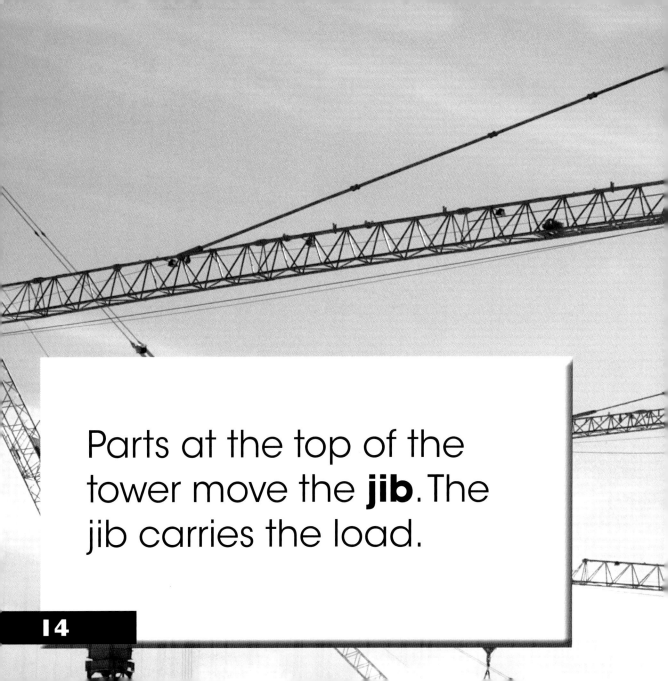

Parts at the top of the tower move the **jib**. The jib carries the load.

15

The jib has a **hook**. The hook picks up the load.

Cables move the jib.
This moves the load.

Cranes must get taller as the buildings rise.

Buildings get built faster with cranes!

WORDS TO KNOW

cab

 hook

jib

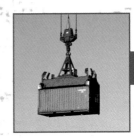 load

INDEX

WEB SITES

Due to the changing nature of Internet links, PowerKids Press has developed an online list of Web sites related to the subject of this book. This site is updated regularly. Please use this link to access the list:
www.powerkidslinks.com/city/cranes/

24